For Nova
with love from
Francis.
Christmas 1980.

BYZANTIUM

BY THE SAME AUTHOR

Poetry

Collected Poems 1960–1984

Plays

Maquettes (a trilogy of one-act plays)
Lying Figures (Part One of REQUIEM, a trilogy)
Killing Time (Part Two of REQUIEM)
Meeting Ends (Part Three of REQUIEM)
A Conception of Love
Light Shadows
Moving Reflections
Living Creation
Healing Nature: The Athens of Pericles
Byzantium

Editor

Eleven Poems by Edmund Blunden
Garland
Studies in the Arts

BYZANTIUM

a play by Francis Warner

Δαρδανικοῖς γὰρ
σκήπτροις Αἰνεαδῶν πᾶσα νένευκε πόλις.

Agathias Scholasticus

OXFORD THEATRE TEXTS 10

COLIN SMYTHE, GERRARDS CROSS, 1990

British Library Cataloguing in Publication Data

Warner, Francis, *1937–*
Byzantium : a play. — (Oxford Theatre Texts,
ISSN 0141–1152; 10)
1. Title II. Series
822'.914
ISBN 0-86140-323-1

Copyright © 1990 by Francis Warner

First published in 1990 by Colin Smythe Ltd.,
Gerrards Cross, Buckinghamshire

Distributed in North America by
Dufour Editions, P.O. Box 449, Chester Springs, PA 19425

Plates of two mosaics in San Vitale, Ravenna, of Justinian and
Theodora by kind permission of © Scala

Cover design and production photographs by Billett Potter of Oxford

Produced in Great Britain
by Billing & Sons Ltd, Worcester

FOR MIRANDA

All enquiries regarding performing rights should be addressed to the publishers.

BYZANTIUM was produced by the Oxford University Dramatic Society (OUDS) for performance in King's College Chapel, Cambridge on Monday, February 12th, 1990, and subsequently in the University Church, Oxford, and in Winchester Cathedral. The play and the production were sponsored by Adamantios Lemos. The director was Tim Prentki.

The cast was as follows:

Justinian	*Tim Hudson*
Cappadocian	*Mark Jolly*
Lydus	*Mark Krais*
Menander	*Dominic Shellard*
Paul	*William Fiennes*
Agathias	*Dougal Lee*
Tribonian	*James Simmons*
Belisarius	*Simon Beaufoy*
Procopius	*Tim Hunter*
Hypatius	*Michael Grenier*
Cosmas	*Barry Webb*
Isdigousnas	*Matthew Whelpton*
Epiphanius	*Michael Grenier*
Spokesman	*James Cannon*
Bodyguards	*Dan Kostopulos*
	Chris Cummings
Priest	*James Cannon*
Theodora	*Bridget Foreman*
Comito	*Sophie Paul*
Antonina	*Anna-Thérèse Lowe*

In Cambridge, Choral Scholars of King's College Choir:
    John Bowley, Martin Eastwood, Robert Rice, Paul Robinson,
    Dan Sladden, Jonathan Wix.

In Oxford and Winchester, St Peter's College Choir, Oxford:
    Jonathan Arnold, Ian Ball, James Lonsdale, Keith Thomasson,
    Oliver Harris, Andrew Johnston, Huw Phillips.

Lighting David Colmer. Electrician Paul Charton. Costumes Penelope Warner with the Royal Shakespeare Company, Oxford Theatre Services, Bradfield College and Kate Blaisdell. Props Clare Daubeney. Assistant to the Director Adrienne Crow. Producers OUDS Presidents Louise Chantal and Richard Long.

Music for Acclamations, etc. in Act One Scene 2 and Act Two Scene 6 was taken from *A History of Byzantine Music and Hymnography* by Egon Wellesz, (Second Edition) Oxford, Clarendon Press, 1961.

Characters

Justinian	*Emperor*
Cappadocian	*Praetorian Prefect*
Lydus	*Praetorian and Chief Secretary*
Menander	*Praetorian*
Paul	*Chief Silentiary and Poet*
Agathias	*Barrister and Poet*
Tribonian	*Quaestor, Minister for Legislation*
Belisarius	*General*
Procopius	*Adviser to Belisarius*
Hypatius	*General, nephew to the late Emperor Anastasius*
Cosmas	*Sea Captain*
Isdigousnas	*Persian Ambassador*
Epiphanius	*Patriarch of Constantinople*
Spokesman	
Theodora	*Empress*
Comito	*Theodora's elder sister*
Antonina	*Wife to Belisarius*

Priests
Bodyguards

The play is set in Constantinople (Byzantium) during the years A.D. 527–548.

There are two acts.

Act One

SCENE ONE

PROCOPIUS
Look, Agathias! As I promised you,
The loveliest sight on earth: Constantine's city,
Rome of the East, behind us, while in front
Two seas rush to embrace and, as they calm
Each other, their bay child, the Golden Horn,
Delights to anchor sleepless pilots' prows,
Smiles to the gardens of Chrysopolis,
And forms a garland round Byzantium.

AGATHIAS
Dear host, Procopius; the clash of seas,
Euxine against Propontis, should create
The roar and thunder of a Persian's boast
Hurled against Rome. These night-left ranks of waves
Gallop and swerve and shy and then retreat
In soft caresses, touch the encircled land,
Then quietly return to curve the bays,
Pleasure the wall-washed, marble-columned city,
And marry Europe into Asia.

PROCOPIUS
Even in violent winter, ruffled ships
Perching this bay are safe. Now April's gleam
Presses the rim of the moon to quench her light
With rays that leap from arch to arch, and wing
Flame-coloured, black and blushed flamingoes north,
Who wade before the morning sun exhausts them,
Homing to lakeside nests. Justinian
Loves to build at the unresting edge, plant deep
Watery foundations, pitting his matchless wealth
Against the penniless sea. Today at last

Act One

The dying Emperor, pushed by the Senate,
Crowns his adopted son — no longer Peter
Sabbatius, old Emperor Justin's nephew,
But Justinianus.

AGATHIAS   Will his Theodora
Join with him in the crown? It is against
All law a prostitute should wear the purple!

PROCOPIUS   Old Justin's wife Euphemia was slave-born,
A foreign ex-concubine, twice market-bought
As Lupicina — illiterate as her husband;
And it was she opposed the circus-girl.
As soon as the Empress died, the Quaestor, Proclus,
Reformed the law: 'A penitent actress may
Apply for an Imperial grant of marriage;
And if the magdalen is blest with one,
All past impediments are washed away.'

AGATHIAS   I see Justinian behind that drafting.

PROCOPIUS   I read your poetry. Your friend, our Paul
Silentiary gives it me to read.
I had forgot you are a barrister.

AGATHIAS   And you are giving up the law!

PROCOPIUS   Not quite.
'Legal adviser to the General,
Young Belisarius' is my new appointment
To go with him on his campaigns, record,
And guide the aftermath of victory.

AGATHIAS   A wide horizon for an advocate.
Listen! The chanting starts!

PROCOPIUS   The coronation,
And a new age begins.

SCENE TWO

The Coronation.

Enter to EPIPHANIUS *the Patriarch and priests (who are before the altar)* JUSTINIAN, *aged 45, dressed in cloth of gold, borne aloft on a shield by five supporters:* CAPPADOCIAN, LYDUS, PAUL, MENANDER, *and* BELISARIUS.

THEODORA, *wearing a chaplet of gold leaves, follows, flanked by* COMITO *and* ANTONINA, *who carry lighted candles.*

As the procession reaches the sanctuary steps it halts. The Patriarch moves formally forward to hold with both hands the edge of the shield. At this point JUSTINIAN *stands up on the raised shield to his full height. The Patriarch steps back, and the shield is slowly lowered to the ground. The bearers step backwards so that all can see* JUSTINIAN *step off the shield. At this point all shout:*

ALL   Vicisti!

The Patriarch blesses the diadem and the purple robes, and, as the KYRIE ELEISON *is sung,* JUSTINIAN, *then* THEODORA, *are robed in the Imperial Purple. All males present bare their heads.* THEODORA *goes to her throne.*

JUSTINIAN *kneels. The Patriarch anoints the head of* JUSTINIAN, *with holy oil, in the form of a cross, saying*:

EPIPHANIUS   In nomine Domini, Patris, Filii, et Spiritus Sancti.

He then says loudly:

Sanctus.

ALL   (*Loudly*) Sanctus!

Act One

EPIPHANIUS Sanctus.

ALL (*Loudly*) Sanctus!

EPIPHANIUS Sanctus.

ALL (*Loudly*) Sanctus!

The Patriarch crowns JUSTINIAN, *and then completes the prayer on his own:*

EPIPHANIUS Dominus Deus Sabaoth. Pleni sunt coeli et terra gloria tua. Hosanna in excelsis. Benedictus qui venit in nomine Domini. Amen.

ALL Amen.

THEODORA *is led from her throne,* COMITO *on one side,* ANTONINA *on the other, to kneel at the sanctuary steps. The Emperor is led to the altar to stand where the Patriarch had stood.* THEODORA, *alone now, rises, walks up the steps to the altar, kneels before her husband, presses her flattened palms together, and places them between those of* JUSTINIAN. *He then crowns her, and says:*

JUSTINIAN Sanctus.

ALL Sanctus!

JUSTINIAN Sanctus.

ALL Sanctus!

JUSTINIAN Sanctus.

ALL Sanctus!

THEODORA *is escorted to her throne by* COMITO *and* ANTONINA.

A gold mantle is now draped over JUSTINIAN. *In his right hand is placed a cross, in his left the Rod of Empire. The Patriarch censes him nine times.*

The Emperor walks the length of the area and back again

so all may see him crowned, with cross and rod in his hands. On his return he bows to the Patriarch, who censes him, then bows in return. The mantle is removed.

EPIPHANIUS May the Lord be mindful of the power of thy kingdom in His universal kingdom, now, and always, and for ever and ever. Amen.

ALL Amen!

The Emperor bows to the Patriarch, then turns and 'accepts' from the Praetorian Prefect a wide plate. The Prefect carries it, heaped as it is with gold coin, as JUSTINIAN, *accompanied by* THEODORA, *slowly moves out at the rear of the procession, flanked by two bodyguards* MENANDER *and* PAUL, JUSTINIAN *scattering gold coins to the people.*

As the couple are about to leave, and all others save the two bodyguards are gone, JUSTINIAN *hands the crown to* PAUL *and says:*

JUSTINIAN Leave us alone awhile.

SCENE THREE

JUSTINIAN Come to my arms, my queen of all the earth!
On this our greatest day I promise you
Before I die to farm and harvest all
This empire till it grows to the far bounds
It felt with Hadrian and the Antonines.
In our religious ceremony, too,
I love the rigour of Chalcedon; but you,
My Monophysite bride, have often said
Rigour must not destroy our granary
Of Egypt, alienate all Syria,
Even if my friend, the Pope, loathes all your sect.

Act One

                    A reconciliation, under God,
                    Of churches Greek and Coptic, Syriac
                    And Latin will be our chief enterprise.

THEODORA   My Emperor, and King! And yet you passed
                    That law against the Arians. You still
                    Hate them, I hope; and will?

JUSTINIAN   Goth heretics.
                    All *Roman* churches. I'll reform the laws!

THEODORA   Make women honoured, give them hope, respect.
                    'Spare the submissive', as our Virgil says —

JUSTINIAN   So does Saint Paul: 'Comfort the down-at-heart.'

THEODORA   You interrupted my quotation. 'Break
                    Rebellion's neck.'

JUSTINIAN   Oh my fierce Queen! I shall.

THEODORA   And hand the poor some access to the courts.
                    I know the wasp of poverty, the sting
                    Of selling love for bread.

JUSTINIAN   It brought you me.

THEODORA   It did, my husband and my whole delight.
                    Now to the Circus Hippodrome where I
                    Began, as worse than nothing, and accept
                    The cringing praise of my old sneering crowd.

JUSTINIAN   In the Imperial Box they all shall see
                    Bruised innocence transfigured into light.
                    So love's urge floods and veers and shadows back,
                    Then all-enveloping blushed morning's hills,
                    Turning to gold the lice on beggars' laps,
                    Flares up time's zodiac to eternity.
                    Your beauty cannot fail to draw their hearts
                    Like seagulls following the harrow.

Byzantium

Fanfare.

THEODORA — Trumpets!

JUSTINIAN — Our four white horses stretch their necks and stamp.
Holding your hand, I shall step out and make
The sign of the Cross on all that circus crowd.
Listen to the cheers! Aspalathus lines the way
With flushed white blossom sweetening the air.
My Theodora, the gold cart arrives.

SCENE FOUR

COSMAS — Please may I speak to you?

TRIBONIAN — Well, I'm not yet Patrician. Merely a lawyer.

COSMAS — What, another? Yet you can talk to me in Greek!

TRIBONIAN — I do;
Though Greek must never be allowed in court.
The Beirut law school where I was enrolled
Goes back to Gaius and the classic age . . .

COSMAS — Of pagans. Well, I am a Christian,
A sea-captain who wants to be a monk,
And so retire into a monastery
To write a book to prove the world is flat.

TRIBONIAN — Good God!

COSMAS — He is.

TRIBONIAN — Haven't you read Aristotle?
He proved earth's round from watching an eclipse.

COSMAS   It's not fine phrases feed the Christian mouth
          But hard-won truths. Look! If I drop this apple,
          It falls as far as it can go; then stops.
          Why is our earth not falling? It's the bottom!
          Air and light go up, and so a vault
          Oblong spans all the rectangle of earth
          Like a rat's cage, or ceiling at the baths.
          The heavens bend down, like four walls, welded
             to
          The corners of the world, beyond the ocean.
          Can you see? There! It's in the Book of Psalms:
          'At thy rebuke the world's foundations were
          Discovered, Lord.'

TRIBONIAN Do you remember how that verse goes on?
          'At the blast of the breath of thy nostrils . . .' Do
             you think
          God's nose gigantic?

COSMAS   You're obscene.

TRIBONIAN   I'm sorry.

COSMAS   Just what is happening in the Hippodrome?
          Last night I beached my prow from India
          (Safely, thank God!) with silk from Selediba —
          An island where they fight perpetual war:
          The Hyacinth King against the King of Trade
          Who rules the harbour and the market-place.
          Before I left, for my last treat, I watched
          A striptease harlot lift her purple dress
          Right off, then make rude noises with her cheeks,
          And laughing call out 'Leda and the Swan!'
          She winked, and lay down naked (bar a string)
          Till tame geese pecked grain off her private parts.
          I saw her there again today; but crowned!

TRIBONIAN You've been away too long. Where is your silk?
          The Emperor himself will buy your bales.
          Will you come to him?

COSMAS — What's your name?

TRIBONIAN — I am Tribonian.

COSMAS — I'm Cosmas. In the Hippodrome
The rival teams are murderous, Blues and Greens.
Which does the Emperor support?

TRIBONIAN — The Blues.

COSMAS — The strip-girl?

TRIBONIAN — Empress!

COSMAS — God forbid!

TRIBONIAN — The Blues;
Though she grew up among the Greens, and fakes
Affection for them when her man requires.

COSMAS — Supporting factions' long hair dangling down
Their backs, shaved foreheads, walrus lips and beards,
(Even at sea I trim mine with fishbones)
Their goose-step, deep bray, boots, and tunic sleeves
Pinched at the wrist then billowing like my sails,
I find barbaric; Hunnic!

TRIBONIAN — Keep remote.

COSMAS — Well, I'll be off.

TRIBONIAN — But how do you explain
Our day and night?

COSMAS — The earth tilts up, North-West,

To a large cone, a mountain. When the sun,
Which is six hundred geographic miles
Across—from here to Alexandria—
(I check mast shadows all times round the year)
When the sun swings behind the cone, it's dark.
If you still think pernicious thoughts, and say
The earth's a sphere—spit! Pagans!—tell me
    this:
Does rain fall upwards in the Antipodes?
I sank you there! (*Exit*)

TRIBONIAN   He'd make a barrister.

SCENE FIVE

PROCOPIUS   Tribonian, my friend from college days
Under that cedar mountain by the sea,
Where old King Kadmos made the alphabet,
And, up past garden fountains, near high streams
Lapped by lithe leopards, 'Solomon' loved Sheba
With cinnamon and honey on his tongue,
Till startled roes and young hinds woke—*your*
    rest!

TRIBONIAN   (*Laughing*) Those were good days. Justinian has
    summoned
Dorotheus our old tutor here,
With Anatolius, for the new commission
On legal education. We must read
Two thousand books, make a *Digest*, and then
Gorge all this into one: a students' text-book:
The *Institutes*.

PROCOPIUS   He's made you chairman?

TRIBONIAN   Yes,
To try the impossible.

PROCOPIUS   Why, everything
Is born afresh with our new Emperor.

Byzantium

Enter LYDUS.

LYDUS I don't like the way, Tribonian,
Procopius, he's cutting back on staff,
And thinning our profession till we lose
All ancient dignities and circumstance.
We've always had the finest scrolls to write on.
Latin, in all our hands, is copperplate—
That handwriting is being dropped in schools.
Incredibly, lawyers now stoop to beg
Thin leaves of grass, trash writing paper, from
The very people who come for advice!
Our robes are fine as our papyrus scrolls.
New ones smell of coin-pinching poverty.
There's even talk of Latin being abolished
And common Greek contaminating courts!

PROCOPIUS None of us three will let the Latin laws
Be prostituted to the vulgar tongue.
And yet, I write my diaries in Greek,
And hope, one day, in a far distant time,
Some Greek-held echo of our dawn will live.

LYDUS Our new dawn has its clouds; my blackest one—
I say this shuddering with rage and loathing—
Praetorian Prefect Cappadocian.
That broad-jowled, lead-jawed, shark-toothed Cerberus
Has chewed my home town, Philadelphia—
Indeed, all Lydia — so fine there's nothing
Left. No people, animals, or cash.
Taxes are forced by torture—in his court
Here's a dark prison trimmed with shackles, irons,
Stocks, and high ropes. It's in use every day.
And then this suction-pump of obols makes
Each victim pay the torturers their wage
For having sweated so hard over him.

TRIBONIAN I do feel somewhat overshadowed by him.
I'm junior to him (though not in age).

	We have to work together — on the Laws. His interest is in economies. (*To* PROCOPIUS) I, too, believe our boiling of the law Won't produce jam till later centuries.
PROCOPIUS	Well, Cappadocian left school when he Had learned to write (not very well). He's pale Because of daily lust continual— Slaves of both kinds are used—and greed for fish. No shrinking scallop, wide-eyed Euxine cod, Translucent sturgeon, shrieking lobster will Be left us! Vomits on his flatterers To eat again. Not till the morning star Can they slide home. No one will work for him.
LYDUS	He's never yet paid me a . . .
TRIBONIAN	Here he comes!

Enter CAPPADOCIAN.

TRIBONIAN	Praetorian Prefect, sir. Your lawyers wait.
CAPPADOCIAN	Good! What were you discussing?
LYDUS	Latin laws.
CAPPADOCIAN	Haven't you the sense to see that, in the East At least, the law courts must go Greek? And will. And you, Procopius?
TRIBONIAN	His diaries.
CAPPADOCIAN	What have you said about me in them? (*Pause*) I've A fair tax, spread on all. As each of us Takes space beneath the sky, it's called 'Sky Tax'. This is on top of normal ones.

PROCOPIUS	For you?
CAPPADOCIAN	Certainly not! For the incumbent's pay (*Smiling*) Of the Praetorian Prefecture.
LYDUS	And Chief Secretary?
CAPPADOCIAN	You? No. When you think The Emperor must fund his latest wars For winning back all the lost provinces, (I'm trying to restrain him, but some priest Says God will make him Lord of Libya) Aristocratic, wealthy men like you Can serve the government for honour. So, Interest rates go up today; and I've Abolished tenure in the Civil Service; The aureus is devalued by one seventh; Freedom of navigation yields to charges At Euxine straits and at the Hellespont; Farm food is requisitioned for the troops; And if you do not like it you can leave.

Exit CAPPADOCIAN.

TRIBONIAN	Able administrator.
PROCOPIUS	Native talent.
LYDUS	It's carefully aimed to soak the upper class!
TRIBONIAN	Sky Tax! The Emperor's honeymoon will pass.

Exeunt.

SCENE SIX

THEODORA	My dearest sister, who taught me to turn The bloom of youth into a scaling-rope, And watched me climb, though never interfered,

Act One

                    And you, promiscuous Antonina dear,
                    Bred in the same trade in the Hippodrome,
                    But relishing the pleasure more than pay,
                    My gifts to you—your husbands—will be here
                    Shortly. How deft three despised 'actresses'
                    Should marry three top self-made Generals!
                    Yours not as old as mine yet, Comito;
                    And yours too young at twenty-five!

ANTONINA   Oh my
                    Belisarius depends on me.
                    He lost his mother young.

COMITO   Generous Empress,
                    My wedding by the Hippodrome to Sittas
                    In your great palace of Antiochus
                    Was refined irony. The Emperor
                    Has asked my husband to seduce the clans
                    North of the Euxine from their Persian strings.
                    Shall I go with him?

THEODORA   You wish to stay chaste?
                    You know your weakness. When you're left alone
                    The shelduck finds a sheldrake.

                    Enter MENANDER.

ANTONINA   What a man!

THEODORA   You may speak, Menander. This boy is
                    Guardsman and bodyguard to both of us.
                    Menander, my imperial sister needs
                    Protection, too. Comito, you may trust him.

COMITO   Didn't I see you in the Hippodrome?
                    What are your hobbies?

MENANDER   Gracious lady, all
                    My interest was in the Blues and Greens.
                    The chariot-race was everything to me—
                    Who rode, who won, whose horses broke their
                        legs.

Byzantium

All my thin income curdled into clothes,
And fighting knives, and girls, and pantomimes.
I even risked death in the wrestling ring.
Whatever decency my father hoped
A legal education would instil
Was spilled in chaos of the weekly fights
Between the factions, and our rioting.

COMITO   A legal education?

MENANDER   Just. My brother,
Herodotus, dropped out. I saw it through,
Then ran. To drift about the Royal Stoa
Hoping some fool would pay my eloquence
In fatuous rhetoric was not for me.

ANTONINA   And so the Emperor made you his guard!

THEODORA   Menander was a Blue. My husband keeps
In touch with those wild swaggerers through him.
He's tough, and he's discreet—and quite
    reformed.

ANTONINA   What a disgraceful life you've led. What fun!
And yet you don't look old . . .

THEODORA   Antonina!
Your husband's here.

SCENE SEVEN

Enter BELISARIUS.

THEODORA   Come, Belisarius.

BELISARIUS   (*Kneeling*) Empress!

THEODORA   Belisarius, you may rise.
We welcome back a hero, girls. This man
At twenty-five has brought a laurel home

Act One

        Not won for many years. In open battle,
        Outnumbered two to one, at Daras all
        The Persian army is defeated by
        The Romans. Am I right?

BELISARIUS   Empress, you are.

THEODORA How did you do it?

BELISARIUS   Mainly cavalry.
       I forced the enemy to attack our wings.
       Our infantry was held back in reserve.
       The wind blew from our side. Oh, various
         things . . .

THEODORA Yes, take your wife. You bring the balm of peace
       To sunburnt thoughts. Soon, tell the Emperor.
       But now close up your ears. Menander! Go!

       Exit MENANDER.

       What I can't stand in Cappadocian
       Is the contemptuous way he croaks me out
       And slimes me to my husband.

COMITO   The Emperor
       Values his skills, but is not influenced.

ANTONINA I've an idea. My Empress, do you want
       His spirit bottled?

THEODORA   His foul perfume plugged?
       I do. Perhaps the Blues and Greens can help.

ANTONINA Well, if that fails, then I'll befriend his daughter,
       Whom I know slightly: Euphemia.

COMITO   Yes,
       A young and gentle girl who tells no tales,
       Though some she could!

THEODORA	I want him so afraid He wakes up screaming, peeps around his door, Lumbers past windows, backs at pillars, peers And hits at darkness, breaking in a sweat Expecting any time the kidney-knife.
BELISARIUS	He works continually against me. Jealousy, I suppose. Some of my men Died, because Cappadocian ordered bread For soldiers not to be cooked twice; just once A little longer—saving on fire-wood, but Wrecking its chance of lasting to the front. When it arrived, it had turned back to flour, Mouldy, vicious, smelling in the sun. A hungry army is an uncaged beast. Fighters must feed.
COMITO	My husband says the same. His answer is to bring clan chieftains home From loyal provinces, and make sure they Are honoured here as members of the Crown Imperial Service, face Cappadocian, And force accountable his wrecking crimes. They'll club that crocodile.

SCENE EIGHT

Enter MENANDER.

MENANDER	Empress, the Emperor.

Enter JUSTINIAN.

JUSTINIAN	My royal partner, and my happiness. Comito, your husband has done well; But you shall stay with Theodora here. Antonina: you shall go to Rome, And Africa. We take your husband's hand In highest honour.

Act One

BELISARIUS (*Kneeling*) All is won for you,
Justinian, my master.

JUSTINIAN And your friend.
Your victory we'll celebrate; but now,
My Empress, you must hear that Antioch . . .

THEODORA Antioch? Why, they're all jokers there,
Hopelessly slack and idle. Their one aim
Is pampered sloth, or the wild Hippodrome.
I don't suppose one soldier stays on guard.

JUSTINIAN There's not much left to protect. Nearly all
The gorgeous buildings rubble. Your idle ones
Blanket in dust and sleep on. An earthquake
Has killed three hundred thousand, and destroyed
The finest of our cities in the East.

COMITO I think we all had friends there.

THEODORA Yes, we did.

JUSTINIAN If the imperial power is to be seen,
And command deference across the world,
It must be by the buildings it creates
To claim the eyes of far posterity.
First, basic needs. Antioch we exempt
From all taxation for three years. We'll build
Again their public monuments and streets,
Fountains and hospitals and theatre,
Stoas and market, sewers and almshouses,
And bend Orontes river round fresh walls.
We'll clear the burned and ruined colonnades
And send what aid our silver ships can bring.

THEODORA You, like a bird, act swiftly, unimpeded,
Fearless against restraining elements,
High above all men, yet the eye of all,
Gifted nest-builder, faithful to our frail homes,
Tireless in brooding all protecting night
Till your dawn song unrolls munificence.
I too will send my best, rebuild the churches

Byzantium

                Guided by you. Wherever accident,
                Famine, catastrophe, or fire strike home,
                Whether the melting snows through Tarsus sweep
                The river Cydnus down the market-place,
                Or Nile forget to go back to her banks
                Rotting all seedlings in their cradle time,
                Wherever lightning strikes, paternal care
                Will compel homage to Justinian
                Till hostile tribes jostle to be your slaves.

JUSTINIAN   My phoenix! Belisarius, before
                We greet the ambassador from the King of Kings
                And hail the beaten crown of Persia,
                Guide us amongst their rocks of hopes and fears.

BELISARIUS   Emperor, we must not forget their king
                Chosroes had been soothed by Roman words
                Even in defeat, though he still smarts that Justin
                Failed to adopt him as his son, when young.
                Persians are not like Romans, nor are they
                Truly barbarians. They do not bury,
                But throw their dead to dogs and birds of prey—
                Yet permit burial to Christians!
                They worship fire—so have a flame beside
                      you—
                Prostrate themselves before the rising sun,
                And will not stamp gold with a human face.
                In battle they rely on cavalry,
                And trembling archers stand on elephants
                Instead of towers. Only long shields protect
                The untrained infantry, poor peasants who
                Are there to strip the corpses, dig, and serve.
                What we can learn from them is how to build
                Bridges in battle. Iron hooks on timber
                      lengths . . .

JUSTINIAN   Enough! Call Isdigousnas. Treat him well
                With every courtesy that's in our power.

BELISARIUS   With him he has his brother Phabrizus,
                His wife, his daughters, and a shoal of slaves.

Act One

JUSTINIAN
: They all shall stay at our expense; but he
Alone may enter here.

SCENE NINE

Enter MENANDER.

MENANDER
: The ambassador
From Persia, Isdigousnas.

Enter ISDIGOUSNAS.

ISDIGOUSNAS
: Emperor Caesar Flavius Justinianus,
God-loved and glorious, famous conqueror
Of nations, ever august, Innovator,
The restless Father of the Roman World;
I stand before you from the King of Kings,
The Persian Monarch, of the Sassan line,
Great son of Kabad: Chosroes the Just,
Who sends you greetings, presents of fine gold,
Peacocks and ivories; and a letter which
Answers all your Rufinus has discussed.

JUSTINIAN
: Greatest of all the kings beyond our throne,
Chosroes' name, and his ambassadors
Will find rich welcome in Byzantium.
What is proposed?

ISDIGOUSNAS
: That you receive our gifts.

JUSTINIAN
: We do; and jewels of Constantine himself
Will travel back with you to Persia.

ISDIGOUSNAS
: Chosroes here proposes Endless Peace
Between the Persian and the Roman world,
On three conditions: Daras never shall
Support a Roman General again
(And, in return, your fort may ever stand);
The Persians rule the farthest Caucasus
And undisturbed lock up the Caspian Sea;

Byzantium

       Thirdly, a royal weight to axle-bend
       Our plume-drawn wagons of eleven thousand
       Pounds in gold shall be the price of peace.
       Your limit-boundary will be secure
       Without a hungry army; while for us,
       Our scholar-King of Kings will then be free
       To bless his subjects through our schools and
         farms,
       And cultivate divine philosophy.

JUSTINIAN Why! This is music Orpheus might have played
       Leading the wild beasts spellbound with his lyre,
       And saving Jason and his Argonauts,
       Coming from Colchis and the Caucasus
       With the gold ram's fleece through our Euxine
         Sea,
       From Siren-whispered song. Yes. We agree,
       And from this day the Endless Truce is born
       Between the greatest kingdoms on this earth.
       Come, dine with us, with all your silken satraps
       Before our treasury fills up your carts.

Exit ISDIGOUSNAS.

       Belisarius, this means we are free
       To win back Africa and Italy.
       Go and prepare the legions! Others may
       See Isdigousnas on his Persian way;
       And when our prancing escorts have come home
       We'll celebrate, and game the Hippodrome!

Exeunt JUSTINIAN *and* BELISARIUS.

SCENE TEN

THEODORA What a strange puffing noise he made, as though
       For empty air he'd sucked a kingdom's wealth.

COMITO   Sister, he seemed the soft epitome
       Of all pretentious Persian villainy.
       Two of his men wore crowns!

Act One

ANTONINA
                                              Our common folk
Think that your husband honours them too
    much.
They use the city as their own; they spy,
Sell, swagger, purchase all that they can buy
Without a single Roman watching them.
What if deception haze their stratagem?

THEODORA
We are at peace now. Think of Pericles.
His city welcomed all and feared no spies,
Was free and open like his character.

ANTONINA
Constantinople is not Athens, nor
Are Persians Greeks.

THEODORA
                             Enough of this. I've heard
Amalasuntha, reigning regent queen
Of all the Gothic kingdom while her son
Lost in debauch has not reached manhood yet;
Amalasuntha, scarcely more than a girl
Herself . . .

COMITO
               She's in her twenties.

THEODORA
                                                 So am I!

ANTONINA
They say she is both beautiful and wise;
Well-educated—of course! Royal blood.

THEODORA
Will you be quiet? Amalasuntha has
Been writing to my husband . . .

ANTONINA
                                           A soft bride.

THEODORA
I'll string you naked by the feet outside
If you provoke my jealousy again!
This dusky Gothic hen has promised him
Welcome in Sicily at Syracuse,
Safe harbour, and a market for the legions.

COMITO
What could be better?

THEODORA	A man who said the same. Yes, she may hand all Italy to him, But he has ordered that Patrician homes In Epidamnus must be strewn for her, For royal progress to Byzantium.
ANTONINA	So golden-hair will be your public guest!
THEODORA	Who said she's blonde?

Enter MENANDER.

MENANDER	My queen, the Emperor asks If you will honour Isdigousnas' wife.
THEODORA	I will. Send word.
ANTONINA	There's no temptation there.
THEODORA	One word more and I'll pluck your every hair.

Exeunt.

SCENE ELEVEN

PAUL *and* AGATHIAS *sitting at a table.*

PAUL	'Each of us loves good wine, so we'll pledge a large bottle to Bacchus, Lover of laughter and cups drowning out man-eating care.'
AGATHIAS	Excellent! Now here is one of mine. 'I was from boyhood disposed to enjoy the heroical metre. Now I collect good verse wreathing my garland of song.'

Act One

PAUL Your garland of song?

AGATHIAS Oh, just a book I'm making.
Your epigrams will form a part, and mine,
And any others we can pluck from friends,
Written in the old manner: some from tombs,
Statues, the old gods—we'll have scurrilous rhymes;
Of course some languid softenings of love;
And boozy quips for dance and partying.

PAUL As at least half my daily time is spent
Enforcing silence round the Emperor
I'll compose hundreds for you, if you like.
'Pleasures in life are few, but the best are when we can abolish
Some of the heart-aching thoughts whit'ning our worrying brows.'
Let's have a competition—each of us
Make one on something—that mosquito net!

AGATHIAS 'Nets are for capturing wings, but I keep them away. They attack me.
Who could be finer than I, saving winged creatures and men?'

PAUL 'Willingly caught in my meshes are men grown drowsy from lunch wine.
I bring the gift of sleep bite-free while freeing the slaves.'

AGATHIAS Your lines grow stronger than mine. Poetry is
A sacred and divinely inspired gift;
Which, as I'm nosing paper in the Stoa
From the first cock until the harbour light
Unravelling legal documents to live,
I have to neglect, like my flute-playing.
I resent such deflection from my dreams.
When there's no work I'm in despair, as taxes
Must be paid, and when there is, I'm sullen.
So if my poems are skimped and undisciplined—
Well, they amuse me, like my tone-deaf singing.

PAUL	But your anthology may fame us all
When our two dusts slide up beams to the sun.
AGATHIAS	You had a brilliant college life; your home's
Ancestral; senatorial parents, yours.
My mother died when I was three. Read this.
It's to her; and in dialogue so I
Can think I speak to her, though—buried—she
Is a forgotten mist through which I see.
PAUL	'Stranger, why do you cry?'
AGATHIAS	'Because you're dead.'
PAUL	'Do you know who I am?'
AGATHIAS	'No, but your end
Saddens me.'
PAUL	'Periclea.'
AGATHIAS	'Who shared your bed?'
PAUL	'A noble Asian husband.'
AGATHIAS	'Why then spend
Eternity beside the Bosphorus?'
PAUL	'Ask Fate.'
AGATHIAS	'And did you leave a son?'
PAUL	'A boy
Of three years old who wanders through the house
Crying for my breasts' milk.'
AGATHIAS	'May he enjoy
A happier life.'
PAUL	'Friend, pray for him, that he
May reach full manhood and shed tears for me.'

SCENE TWELVE

Enter JUSTINIAN.

JUSTINIAN My friends, two poets. How's Tribonian?
Are they hurrying on with no delays
Distilling down our heritage of laws,
Pruning and cutting so new buds may spread
And the strong branches hold? Agathias—
No immortality from idleness.

AGATHIAS Emperor, we were sharing poetry.
The *Digest* has been forced to pause.

JUSTINIAN   Slow down
The urgent enterprise by which we shall
Preserve, renew, and hand on Rome's great gift
To future ages?

AGATHIAS   Cappadocian,
The master of that ship, is blown off course
To fish in other seas. He must raise funds
To finance the Lost Territories War.

JUSTINIAN Now Persia's melted from us, we have strength
To hoist the Vandals from North Africa
And rescue Dido's city, build again
That circuit wall and ramparts, recreate
The aqueduct. All Romans shall be free
From Colchis and the Caspian Gates, through
    Susa,
Down to the plains of India; through deserts
Egyptian, where vast Karnak Pharaohs stand
Dwarfing a past that awed Herodotus;
Up through our loyal Numidia of the Moors,
Over the waves to welcoming Sicily.
From Rome, Ravenna, Tuscany, the Alps
We'll toss the Arian heretics across
Hannibal's snows, and dance those Goths far
    North.

Impossibility is not our word,
For we'll reach round and unslave sandwashed
    Spain,
Lift from great Hercules the pillars that
Uphold the world—beyond which no man sails—
And grip a continent in either hand
To kiss our peace across that slender sea.

AGATHIAS   Justinian, can we afford the cost?

JUSTINIAN   Our Vandal plunder will finance our men,
And the taxation from new provinces
Will more than recompense us. What's the poem?

PAUL   On a mosquito net.

JUSTINIAN   Is that the best
Use of your gifts from God? I've written one
To show the sufferings of Christ on earth
The Son felt in the Holy Trinity.
Our Patriarch, one hundred years ago
In our own city here, denied that truth.
'Only-begotten Son and Word of God,
Who, being Immortal, yet wast pleased to be
For our salvation made incarnate from
Blest Mary, Ever-Virgin, Mother of God,
And without change wast made man, for our
    sakes
Crucified, trampling Death by your own death;
O Christ our God, Son of the Trinity,
Glorified with the Father and Holy Spirit,
Save us.'

AGATHIAS   Souls in a state of inspiration,
As Plato taught us, those who are possessed
With divine frenzy from the Muse, give birth
To children of unfading loveliness.

PAUL   And your philosophy, my Emperor,
Is sound; much needed.

Act One

JUSTINIAN	My philosophy?
Theology, dear boy! Now, Agathias,
If I did not know you were orthodox
I'd ask 'Why Plato?' Too long we've ignored
Athens' and Alexandria's pagan ways.
'More threat from heresy than pagan gods',
You'll say; and that is true: but it is two
Centuries since Julian forbade
Christians to teach the classics. Now, shall I?
In Alexandria we hold the strings
As academic salaries are paid
By us. Athens' Academy was endowed
By Plato. Interest on a thousand years
Has given them independence.

PAUL	Plato's garden
Was all he left; and that was only worth
Three gold coins.

JUSTINIAN	But ten thousand benefactions
Have made it Croesus-rich. Damascius
Their scholiarch, and many pupils who
Love him and follow him: Simplicius, Isidore,
Olympiodorus, Priscian and the rest—
Are active pagans, and attract the best
Minds in the Empire!

PAUL	Anti-Christians!
Bean-eating Athenians! Yet who could
Lecture as well as they can?

AGATHIAS	The new law
You've drafted says no pagans now may teach.
Will that include the universities?

JUSTINIAN	It will and does; and those endowments which
Protect the pagans from the Living Word
Of Christ, and lead impressionable minds
To study Proclus, magic, rain-making
And all pre-Christian paganism past,
We'll requisition. Alexandria
Obeys. The Athens colleges will close.

AGATHIAS	Great Emperor, it was not for a wreath
Of parsley or wild olives that fine men
Entered the Olympic and Nemean Games.
They looked for glory, deathless and divine.
So too our soldiers risk their limbs and lives
Not for evaporating plunder, but
To earn a name through generations hence.
Can the long-cherished gold that we so need,
Taken from the Athenian colleges,
Outweigh the curse of future centuries?
'Justinian destroyed what Plato gave.'
JUSTINIAN	Back to your *Digest*! I shall leave a name
Carved in ten thousand buildings, which will live
To be, like Solon, praised to farthest time
As his who gathered in the endless laws.
The Word of Christ dissolves the Academy!
St Paul saw Athens in idolatry,
And on Mars Hill he drew no salary.
PAUL	Yes; Solon combined laws with poetry . . .
JUSTINIAN	One day you'll write a Christian poem; for me!

Exeunt.

SCENE THIRTEEN

PROCOPIUS	The crowds are ugly. Cappadocian
Provokes them. They say family settlements
And wills cannot be trusted with him. Tax
Exemption he abolishes; and they blame
Tribonian, too, our courteous digester.
But Cappadocian's is the neck they gnaw.
LYDUS	Small wonder! When I came here Zoticus
Was the Praetorian Prefect. He gave me
My first job—we both came from Lydia.
In my first year I made one thousand gold
Pieces: legally! So I was grateful,

Act One

                Wrote him a panegyric—far too short,
                Because he told me to go to the bank
                And draw one gold coin for each written line.

PROCOPIUS   Isn't your wife his daughter?

LYDUS   Best of women,
                Virtuous, discreet; brought me a wedding shower
                Of naked gold that weighed one hundred pounds.

PROCOPIUS   A Prefect's yearly African salary!

LYDUS   Not bad for a young man of twenty-two.
                But listen! I don't understand the mob.
                They plead that violence between the Blues
                And Greens inside the city walls be crushed.
                Justinian, though he favours the Blues,
                Demands impartial punishment for all
                Offenders; rightly. Eudaemon the Prefect
                Condemns seven hooligans from both the clubs
                To be paraded in the streets, then killed.
                Four were beheaded, one hanged; but the two
                Remaining, one a Green and one a Blue,
                Dropped from the scaffold live. St Conan's monks
                Shipped them to sanctuary. Now the cry
                Uniting both the factions, against us,
                Is to have both reprieved.

PROCOPIUS   They care for nothing—
                Country, marriage, God, or their own lives;
                Nothing except these factions. Diseased souls.
                I cannot understand fanatic fans.
                Justinian must face the Hippodrome
                In person. Nothing else will tranquil them.

                Exeunt.

SCENE FOURTEEN

JUSTINIAN   Anthemius asks if we'd like to view
                The low-pitched dome of our new private chapel.

COMITO	Oh, sister; may I come too?
THEODORA	It's a secret Place.
JUSTINIAN	My jewelled love-knot, twined in stone Round Theodora's heart. Our sacred nest.
THEODORA	We'll walk a private path, secure from sight Of the drunk crowd, myrtled with evergreen, To where Anthemius' church of our two saints Holds to this palace like a mother's breast.
JUSTINIAN	Not a basilica, but small, and new— An octagon that's domed . . .
THEODORA	Our two names carved Above acanthus capitals that swirl Their tendrils in my hair-style . . .
JUSTINIAN	Deep-cut lace Hexameters the cornice architrave, Linking our names in verse for all time. Come!

Enter MENANDER.

MENANDER	My lord, I never dreamed the hating factions Would blend their discontent, but now both yell 'Long live the humane Greens and Blues!' Both want Their half-hanged colleagues pardoned. They have burnt The prisons, freed the cells and killed the guards— Though monks hold those two past the Golden Horn— And Saint Sophia is burning!
JUSTINIAN	Start the games! Set the fast chariots racing! I have said To all that crowd I will not pardon them.

Act One

SCENE FIFTEEN

Enter BELISARIUS.

BELISARIUS Emperor, may I . . .

JUSTINIAN Speak, Belisarius.
What do the raving Manichaeans demand?

BELISARIUS They shout out 'Nika!' 'Conquer!' Your Bronze
    Gate
Of the Palace burns now! The Zeuxippon baths
And seating planks piled in the Hippodrome . . .

JUSTINIAN Which end?

BELISARIUS The North end, by the burning
    baths.
The Augusteum and the Senate House
Light up the black sky as they crack to ash.

JUSTINIAN The Senate! All for two criminals?

BELISARIUS New names
Have moved among the factions, urging on
Demands that come from Senatorial minds.

JUSTINIAN *goes out on to balcony.*

PAUL Silence! Silence! Hear your Emperor!

JUSTINIAN Half of the city is in flames! Your homes!
Will you please give me peace to answer you?
One of you speak for all. What do you want?

SPOKESMAN You sack the City Prefect, who condemned
Our friends. Throw out the Cappadocian
Who bleeds us dry and throws all out of work;
And that smart law-changer, Tribonian!

JUSTINIAN You want these three removed from public office?

CROWD	Nika! Nika! Nika! Nika! Nika!
PAUL	Silence! The Emperor answers!
JUSTINIAN	On these four Gospels illuminating sacred truth I give my oath I strip their power today.
CROWD	(*Great cheer*)
SPOKESMAN	You gave an oath to stammering Vitalian When he voiced grievances. And did you keep it?
CROWD	Perjurer! Long live Hypatius! Long live Old Emperor Anastasius' nephew!

JUSTINIAN *returns from balcony.*

JUSTINIAN	Hypatius! Last night I sent him from this palace, home. He was so keen to stay, I could not feel His motives were just loyalty.
MENANDER	(*Looking outside*) The crowd Carry him from the Forum of Constantine Dressed in your robe, a collar on his head.
JUSTINIAN	My clothes?
BELISARIUS	Not all your Palace Guard are loyal. Someone threw out your purple cloak to them.
MENANDER	Now in the Hippodrome they lift him to The Imperial Seat, your Kathisma!
JUSTINIAN	Menander, Take coin and give, quietly, to all the Blues Enough to buy them silently away. Hypatius loves the Greens. Remind them. Warn! Then return back to Belisarius.

Exit MENANDER.

Act One

BELISARIUS My private army, mainly Gothic troops,
Are loyal to me.

CROWD (*Shouting outside*) Hypatius Augustus! Hypatius
Augustus!

JUSTINIAN Reach for Hypatius
And bring him to me here. Take Mundus with
you.
His Heruli men defend the Danube well.
A few are in town with him. As little blood
Spill as you can; but order must be forced.
If I'm not here, I'll leave word where I am.
Go, Belisarius! Genius of the wars!
Scatter like pigeons all who leap our laws!

Exit BELISARIUS.

SCENE SIXTEEN

Enter CAPPADOCIAN.

JUSTINIAN John Cappadocian . . .

CAPPADOCIAN The fleet is manned,
And loyal. I've stuffed treasure through the ships.
They rock on tranquil waves at anchor where
Your palace garden steps finger the sea.

PAUL Yes, cross to Heraclea for a time . . .

THEODORA My Emperor?

JUSTINIAN Not now.

CAPPADOCIAN What is it, woman?

THEODORA My Lord; forgive my words. To those who hold
No woman ought to dare assert herself
When men deliberate, or cringe in fear,

I answer that this present crisis needs
The best solution, from whatever mind.
Each of us born into the light must die,
But for an Emperor to turn and run
To live in exiled, powerless vanity
Is unendurable. I pray that I
May never yield the purple, know that day
When those who meet me do not call me
    'Queen'.
Caesar, if you decide to save yourself,
There is the sea. Your ships are waiting;
    crammed.
But, leaving, ask: is not a glorious death
More splendid than wretched security?
I was not educated, yet I know
A saying which may be my epitaph:
'Royalty is a noble burial shroud.'

JUSTINIAN   That's why I chose you as my Empress. All
You rabbit-hearted comforters, hear her!
She has a Roman's courage, mastering Fate
To transform defeat into victory.
Some people are, as others strive to be,
Their chosen image. Here, at vanishing point,
Exhilaration turns us round, and see!
The evidence remains, the structure holds.
The past is always present. We create
A future from our follies. Half-reaped wheat
Of possibility can harvest us!
So keep your thoughts and senses nimble; dream,
Then tap the notion with your own reflection
Until it bodies out into the world
Of action, and new days look back to now
In awe and wonder. We are men, and still
Spirits impregnable that comprehend
The sweep of time, the scattered, gleaming stars,
The coral seas from snow to camelled sands,
The claw of winter and soft April days,
Lilies, each shivering insect, elephants,
Our bodies' rhythms, and those greater truths
No libraries can hold of nature's ways

            And ever-changing process, of which we
            Are one brief, fading spark, yet grasp it all,
            Confined, yet wholly free before night falls,
            Because our minds, unlimited, create
            The very God who made us in His image,
            Sin and salvation jostling for free-will
            Like blackberries blown in September winds
            On their own thorns, and bleeding drop. We shall
            Rule and recover, build a greater church
            To Holy Wisdom, for remotest time
            To understand our gratitude for life.

                        SCENE SEVENTEEN

            Enter BELISARIUS *with* HYPATIUS, *dressed in*
            JUSTINIAN'*s purple robe.*

JUSTINIAN   Hypatius, why have you traitored me?

HYPATIUS   My Lord, it was to gather in one place
            All of your enemies.

JUSTINIAN   You have done well.
            If you had such authority, why wait
            To use it until half my city's burned?

HYPATIUS   The people led us there against our will.
            Yet we who are about to die won't weep:
            But spare my family.

JUSTINIAN   I shall.

            Exit HYPATIUS *stripped of the purple, under guard.*

BELISARIUS So many dead, my Emperor; so many!
            My Goths, and Mundus' Heruli, carnage on
            The panicked dying in the Hippodrome.

JUSTINIAN   Command them stop! No massacre can heal
            The wounds this city weeps. Bring them to heel!

Exit BELISARIUS.

My hubris is rebuked. God knows what grief
Thousands will feel tonight. Our grim relief—
To announce victory, for what it's worth;
And then rebuild in sorrow a new birth.

END OF ACT ONE

Act Two

SCENE ONE

PROCOPIUS (*Formally, to audience*)
Seven hundred years have passed since Scipio
At Zama conquered Africa, and won
The title 'Africanus'. Now our son
Of New Rome, here today, whose overthrow
Of Vandal Carthage makes our Empire grow
By a whole continent, which every one
Of us may call our own, has just begun
His Triumph to the Hippodrome. Look! Slow,
On foot, from his own house, leading great King
Gelimer of the Vandals, with a band
Of prisoners, fair and tall. Barbarian
Treasures that blaspheme eyesight, everything
The Vandals plundered, placed now in the hand
Of Belisarius for Justinian.

AGATHIAS (*Formally, to audience*)
Our Africanus at the throne kneels low.
Justinian stands with Theodora, none
In their Kathisma but these two. Undone,
Gelimer's stripped and prostrated, on show.
The last King of the Vandals feels the blow,
Cries: 'All is vanity beneath the sun!'
But does not weep. Victor, and vanquished one,
Kneeling, and prone, touch purple from below.
Across the Hippodrome goes echoing
A roar that's heard in every Roman land
As freedom's granted to the Arian.
The Vandal suppliants are carrying
Their conqueror, made Consul, as was planned
For Belisarius by Justinian.

SCENE TWO

ANTONINA   My glowing Queen!

THEODORA   Our husbands have done well.
This year brings golden harvest from our seeds
Sown in sheer faith against advice of all.
Your Belisarius scatters Vandal spoil
Among the crowd as Consul, while the suave
Tribonian—now safely reinstated
In his old job (with Cappadocian, too;
That's not so good)—presents the Emperor
With their completed *Digest* of the laws—
A task impossible as in six months
Subduing Africa! But both by God
Willed into being through us. That great dream
Of universal peace restored all round
The Mediterranean, through the Roman world,
Administered from this foundation-stone
Of lasting justice both for rich and poor,
Wakes into daylight, proves our vision true.

ANTONINA   What did the Emperor say to Gelimer?
We saw he gave him freedom.

THEODORA   Would you say
That magnanimity's the poise of greatness?
My husband gave him, in Galatia,
Imperial garden walks with peacock pools,
Lions in light bronze that move their heads and
    claws,
And roar; a place where nightingales weave notes
On palace walls that house his family;
And wealth enough to weary out his days.
Had he been willing to renounce his creed
Of Arius, that Christian heretic,
We would have made him a Patrician.

ANTONINA	He'd rather live Galatian luxury Playing the lyre, and sponging his weak eyes.

Enter JUSTINIAN.

JUSTINIAN	Good news, my Queen! Good news from Italy!
THEODORA	Did you send Peter the Illyrian, The gentle, soft-voiced diplomat, alone To Amalasuntha and Theodahad?
JUSTINIAN	To find out why her treasure ship arrived In Epidamnus harbour, then hoist sail Back to Ravenna, where it idly waits Bobbing the waves as sailors fish and dice, And time goes by. She hands the Gothic power Of Italy to us, now her son's dead.
ANTONINA	Athalaric is dead?
JUSTINIAN	From a debauch.
ANTONINA	Who then is king?
JUSTINIAN	She shares the power with That greedy intellectual Theodahad, Her only relative that's male. She once Stripped him of lands he stole in Tuscany, So won the Tuscans' love. Now she needs him If she—a woman—is to stay in charge, And from Ravenna rule all Italy.
ANTONINA	I hope he shares her generosity.
JUSTINIAN	We'll see. Bring in Amalasuntha's letter Peter sent on ahead! Africa, Italy, The *Code*, the *Digest*, and the *Institutes* . . . Every impossible project triumphs home! Why are you silent?

Letter is brought in by MENANDER. JUSTINIAN *reads it.*

Act Two

THEODORA   I admire, my Prince,
Your zest in luck and courage in defeat.
You are the Father of all Flocks; as smoke
Drives away bees, so your name rules the seas.

ANTONINA   He seems preoccupied, and angry.

JUSTINIAN   What
Is this? She has been strangled in her bath?
Theodahad swore he would keep her safe
Or risk my wrath. Young, soft, so beautiful,
Nakedly hand-clasped, kicking out for life,
Wet, without prayers or priest, her women
    fled!
Who could have counteracted my demand?
What power is higher than the Imperial Seal
Save God alone? Paul! Call my ministers
To the great Palace, on the mosaic floor
Where conquered portraits of our enemies
Mingled with fighting beasts are daily trod.
My Beauty, this means war against the Goths
Till in Ravenna's very heart we build
Our own imperial church for Italy
To render thanks to God for victory.
We'll dream it from our private chapel here,
But loftier, awe-inspiring, light, and fresh;
Send the same craftsmen, hack the quarries bare
Of Proconnesus—pure, grey marble for
Columns and capitals carved in our style
Resting on patterned floors that meadow round
An arch of honour through which kings will creep
To where, flanking the altar, on each wall,
Two masterpieces of mosaic art
Compel each earthbound prayer for us to heaven.
You, on the South, my Empress, pearled and
    crowned
Offer the golden chalice. Opposite,
A matchless portrait in imperial robes,
With priests and generals, of your true love
Crowned, nimbused in heaven-touched
    divinity.

Exit JUSTINIAN.

ANTONINA He is creative in his rage; and yet—
         It seems a little odd you would not speak?

THEODORA What's in your guess you may not think or tell.
         I'll need my old skills if all's to be well!

         Exit THEODORA.

                    SCENE THREE

ANTONINA Menander!

         Enter MENANDER.

MENANDER   Madam, I am here.

ANTONINA   Why not
         Guarding the Emperor?

MENANDER   Others are. I act
         As diplomat as well as bodyguard.

ANTONINA You must see much that you can never tell.

MENANDER All palaces have secrets.

ANTONINA   Don't I know!
         But you, full-bodied boy, have never married?

MENANDER You know my days were spent among the Blues,
         And faction fornication.

ANTONINA   So were mine.
         A good start! Chrysostom the saint has said
         'If marriage is delayed for a young man,
         He finds a taste for flippancy and farce,
         Laughter, licentiousness, and liberty.'
         It's hot. Do slip that belt off.

Act Two

MENANDER   It holds up
My trousers.

ANTONINA   Never mind. Neither of us
Is innocent. Yes, do. Now, leaving this,
Tell me. I didn't know diplomacy
Was your responsibility at times.
Do you know Peter the Illyrian?

MENANDER   Madam, your . . . !

ANTONINA   Back. Please rub it. Ah!
Just there.

MENANDER   Well, yes. I saw him to his leaving ship—
It was my job to help him on his way—
And I remember: just before he made
His formal embrace and climbed up the plank,
A message in a sewn-up envelope
Bearing the Empress' seal was rushed to him.

ANTONINA   I'd not say anything of that at all
To anyone. See?

MENANDER   Well, now he's returned
He's been promoted by the Empress far
Beyond the other career diplomats.

ANTONINA   Yes, that off, too.

Enter BELISARIUS.

BELISARIUS   Wife! Antonina! Am
I interrupting? Have I to pretend

Exit MENANDER.

The evidence of my own eyes deceives me?

ANTONINA   Belisarius, I do not like your mind;
Crude and suspicious. I'm stung by a wasp.

Byzantium

He's calmed the inflammation, as I urged,
And tells me we are off to Italy!

BELISARIUS   If, in the wars, some success has been mine
Much more through God's gift than my
    craftsmanship
Of strategy, my part—I hope—has been
Discretion, and right judgement of events.
With you alone I lose that power to know
True from the false. Time conquers all, save love.
Strength, beauty, youth, yes, life itself, are locked
Swiftly into the passing cart of weeks
Like fear-eyed calves to slaughter, soon forgot.
When love is infinite, it cannot be
Dungeoned in days, but transforms everything
It touches into value and delight.
My Antonina, I must go to fight
The Gothic king, and take the Western shores
Northward from Rome until Ravenna's ours.

ANTONINA   Then take my Photius.

BELISARIUS   Your son from your last
Marriage? I will. He's still to grow his beard,
But has firm character beyond his age.
He'll be accepted, since he is our own,
And can control finance with honesty.

ANTONINA   I show my love in deeds, not words. Do you
Remember, while we sailed the Adriatic
Against the Vandals, the whole fleet becalmed
At sea, and water on the ships turned foul
Because the sunlight burned it into slime—
Your Massagetae restless as you had
Impaled two on sharp stakes for drunken murder?
(Their home laws make drunk killing a light
    crime.)
I hid the jars in darkness in the hold,
Buried in sand, and kept the water clean?

BELISARIUS   I do, my love. But this time you must stay.
Protect the Empress. Think of us; and pray.

Exeunt.

SCENE FOUR

JUSTINIAN Lawyers, before I leave you to your work,
Hear my new edict. I, as head of state
And church, lay down guidelines for heretics—
Most of whom follow down from Arius:
Nestorians, Monophysites, Aphthartodocetists.
'In the Name of our Lord Jesus Christ,
The Emperor Caesar Flavius Justinianus,
Conqueror of the Alamanni, Goths, and Franks,
Germans, Alani, Vandals, Africans,
Pious, happy, glorious, ever august:
We say the greatest blessing for mankind
Is full confession of the Christian faith,
True, universally acknowledged by
All priests worldwide, in unity and peace.
Our power ratifies the deposition
Decree pronounced against hard Severus,
To whom we've been too tolerant too long.
Severus, the Monophysite monk,
Bringer of discord into Holy Church,
Is anathematized. We here forbid
Any to read his writings. Every work
Of his is to be burnt. He may not come
To this Imperial City. None may hear
Him speak, pass on his thoughts or words. Those who
Make copies, fair or rough, will lose one hand
By amputation. Severus must find
Some lonely desert to complete his days.'
I'll leave the rest with you. If war is won
And holy peace installed, the Empire will
Flourish as under Marcus Aurelius.

Exit.

TRIBONIAN That may not make for peace at home: in the Imperial bed!

Byzantium

PROCOPIUS Though Theodora still
Protects the Monophysites, she is less
Successful than when, under her strange spell,
The Emperor chose for our patriarch
Anthimus of Trapezus.

AGATHIAS He professed
The Monophysite faith of Theodora,
Bringing Pope Agapetus here in rage
To make sure that our patriarch was deposed.

LYDUS He didn't last long. Nowadays too many
Draft documents about which they have no
Idea, and are completely ignorant.

PROCOPIUS I know the subtleties of the disputes,
But I'll keep quiet. It's madness to me,
Folly presumptuous, to search out God's mind
When who can understand our oddities?

AGATHIAS What is the news from the Italian war?

LYDUS Whatever it is means cash must be found.
Justinian's still cutting back on staff,
And now the great work is complete suggests
I, with some other lawyers, go to teach!

TRIBONIAN He'll go on altering the laws. He needs
Good Christians in the universities.
You should be flattered!

AGATHIAS Lydus, you'd teach well!
I'd give up law tomorrow, just to write
'And mingle Graces with the Muses' as
Euripides once said. Today, I am
Deeply depressed because my cat has chewed
The head off my poor partridge. I pulled free
The body, and have dug it a deep grave
So that my cat can't scoop it from the tomb.

LYDUS It takes so long to climb the Civil Service,

Act Two

> To which I've given my life so far, that all
> Department Heads are senile, and are run
> By junior clerks and secretaries, while we
> Who know the job are axed at prime.

TRIBONIAN
>   It's all
> Economies. But what news from the war
> We're paying for, Procopius?

PROCOPIUS
>   Our Mundus
> Is dead, defeated in Dalmatia.
> Germanus has suppressed the mutiny
> In Africa. Theodahad's deposed,
> And his usurper Vitiges confronts
> Our Belisarius under siege in Rome.

LYDUS
> I hear they kill the mules for sausages,
> And live on herbs and nettles . . .

TRIBONIAN
>   Why, you can
> Tell us your own experience!

PROCOPIUS
>   I can.
> Sixteen sailing days with helpful wind
> Have brought me home. Water and famine rule.
> Yet Belisarius is in control.

AGATHIAS
> Your diaries will far outlive us all.
> When can we share them? Ah! Tribonian.
> Your garrulous sea-captain's back again.

Exeunt all except TRIBONIAN.

SCENE FIVE

Enter COSMAS.

COSMAS
> Sorry I'm late. I was distracted by
> A whale.

TRIBONIAN   A whale!

COSMAS   Yes, on the beach down by
             Sagaris river. You know how deep it is,
             And how it rushes down so fast no one
             Has ever bridged it! Well; miraculous calm
             Settled, and brought the housewives out to stare
             At myriad dolphins leaping in delight.
             Then suddenly Porphyrius appeared,
             Deceived by the calm water, I suppose.

TRIBONIAN   Porphyrius! Who's capsized endless ships
             For fifty years? The Emperor has offered
             A reward for his capture.

COSMAS   Someone's rich.
             His vast mouth swallowed dolphins like sardines
             And could not stop, although he can't have been
             Hungry by now, but chased them until beached
             In stuck mud. He jerked, struggled, writhed, and
                hammered
             With his tail, but just sank deeper down.
             Everyone rushed with furious axes, knives,
             To hack him, but he would not die. They pulled
             Some heavy ropes from drying ships, and dragged
             The whale slowly up on wheels. Some ate
             The flesh raw; others, careful like myself,
             Cured it in smoke. I have some. Take a piece!

TRIBONIAN   I here acknowledge an historic bite.
             The Emperor will see you. Give him some!

             Enter JUSTINIAN.

JUSTINIAN   Tribonian; I've made you a Patrician.

TRIBONIAN   My profound thanks. I love the classical,
             Old institutions. They had fallen away,
             Declined through imperial neglect, but now
             Under the cloudless sun of your great sky
             They are restored.

JUSTINIAN   But not unthinkingly.
          Law is like medicine, we find what works,
          What helps to heal, drawn from the old and new.
          We build, discard, discover, modify
          Always for fairness and simplicity
          To practical and Christian ends. Who's this?

TRIBONIAN My sea-captain I told you of, with silk
          And whale meat.

COSMAS   Mighty Emperor and King,
          Cosmas is my name.

JUSTINIAN   Cosmas! Come, sit down.
          You sail the seas—what whale meat have you
               brought?
          Is it from beached Porphyrius?

COSMAS   It is!

JUSTINIAN He was Leviathan. No spear could hurt him!
          Another treachery to Romans gone.
          I'll try it later. Have you silk to sell?

COSMAS   My ship's load.

JUSTINIAN   I will buy at fifteen gold
          Pieces for each pound of silk. We need
          Silk desperately. All we buy is from
          The Persians; and that's an embarrassment.
          Where is it from?

COSMAS   Selediba, where trade
          From the Far East comes west. There's Chinese
               silk,
          Indian aloes, cloves, and sandalwood,
          Malabar pepper, Sindu musk and castor,
          Soft and bright copper from Kalliana . . .

JUSTINIAN   Stop!
          How can I buy more silk?

Byzantium

COSMAS   Emperor, you need
An expert who can understand their ways.
Shopping's not easy. When the Axomite
King needs gold, his traders take lump salt
And travel to the mines in frankincense
Country. They make a camp; circle it round
With a high hedge of thorns. They settle in,
Slaughter the oxen, lay that meat on thorns,
With the salt lumps, and wait. The natives come,
Leave golden pellets on the flesh—or salt—
And then retire. If the selling Axomites
Are satisfied, they take the gold and leave
The meat—or salt. If not, they leave it till
The natives tiptoe back and put some more
Or collect back the gold they left. It works.

JUSTINIAN   It's slow.

COSMAS   But typical.

JUSTINIAN   Can no one speak
Their language?

COSMAS   Few. Remember, if you go,
When sailing, dolphin meat's like pork, but dark
In colour; smelly. Seal is white and clear.
Turtle and dolphin? Cut their throats; but seals
We normally club on the head.

JUSTINIAN   But silk!

COSMAS   Ah, yes. You've heard I want to be a monk,
(As good Tribonian knows) for excellent reasons?
I have two friends who're monks—you can't buy silk
From Indians, if that's your thought. The Persians
Control the harbours where the Indian ships
Arrive, and buy all cargoes.

Act Two

JUSTINIAN   Monks.

COSMAS   My friends
Might help you grow silk here. I don't know how—
And yet I know the secret's mulberry leaves . . .

JUSTINIAN   Do you know what you're saying? That the scarce
Elegant luxury all Romans crave,
Which throws us into debt with Persia, both
In peace and war, you think just might grow
    here?
The source of that rare weave that elevates
Our highest women; with which I must dress
All ministers of state, ambassadors;
Hand down to gratify new-bending kings
To prove Imperial favour?

COSMAS   Mulberry leaves,
That's it. I don't see why . . . Look! I have seen,
Once, a rhinoceros—a good way off!
I've seen a dead one stuffed with hay and straw.
His skin's four fingers thick, which farmers use
Instead of iron in their ploughs; it's cheaper.
His horns grow stiff to root up trees and fight
The elephant . . .

JUSTINIAN   No more! No more. If you
Can bring your two monk friends to me . . .

COSMAS   Will you
Make me a monk so I can write my book?

JUSTINIAN   I will; and you shall live in luxury
If this creates our own silk industry.

Exit COSMAS.

Tribonian, I must ride to church in state,
And Saint Sophia's rebirth celebrate!

Exeunt.

SCENE SIX

In Hagia Sophia.

LYDUS
Where were you when you heard the murder of
Queen Amalasuntha?

AGATHIAS
                    Watching a full moon
Of warm translucence that bathed in the sea
Of Marmora, while I stood high above
The Golden Gate of Theodosius;
Below me, the new gate Justinian
Built to embrace the conquering legions home
From Belisarius' African victory.

PAUL
I? At the Egyptian obelisk that same
Theodosius the Great set up
Finding it lying in the shrubberies,
Dragged long before from Karnak, now reared high
Commemorating all his victories,
To dominate the Hippodrome.

MENANDER
                        The women
Believe it's magic and can heal.

TRIBONIAN
                            And I
Was in the Hippodrome, too, at the serpents'
Column, twisted from the melted bronze
Weapons defeated Persians left behind
At Plataea. Our Constantine himself
Brought it to us from Delphi.

PROCOPIUS
                        I was under
The aqueduct of Valens; but today
We shall remember all our lives. The builders
Anthemius and Isidorus have
Created here a mystery of light
Dwarfing past monuments as mountain peaks

Act Two

Stunt hills, for great Justinian. The riots
Deliver here a far more lasting crown
For Christ than any dreamed. This climbs the
   sky!
Look! Like a great ship sailing on the land
Sophia lifts the city's thoughts, and frowns
All eyes that peer up at a dome suspended
By a gold chain from Heaven.

MENANDER
                            The Emperor
Rides in on a white horse! Dismounts. He comes
To where the throne within its circles marks
The centre of the world.

Enter JUSTINIAN.

JUSTINIAN
                            In praise of God,
And adoration of His majesty,
I thank my architects: Anthemius
Whose skill, with Isidorus, gives us this
The greatest church the world has ever seen.
Solomon! I have surpassed you! But
Not unto us, not unto us the praise,
O God, but unto Thee, who at this time
Of Christmas came born in a cave and, cold,
Cried in the straw of animals for milk.
Two poets lead the celebrations. First,
Grave Romanus, once deacon in Beirut,
Now honoured writer of one hundred hymns
We know and love. You lead the singing. There,
From the curved pulpit, Paul Silentiary,
Read your rich epic written for this day
Describing our new glittering house of God
To future ages, so they bend the knee
Constantinoplewards, to our seven hills,
And crawl the world to worship and admire.
Come, Patriarch. Begin! Paul, read to us!

PAUL
First let us thank in joy the divine and
   omnipotent Master
Architect, holy above, and his echo our Almighty
   Monarch
Justinianus Caesar . . .

Byzantium

        ROMANUS's *hymn takes over.*

PAUL   Now the great morning has come, and the huge door groans on its hinges
Welcoming Caesar, Queen Theodora, who lead in their subjects,
Driving away dark shadows with dawn, so whoever looks up high
Far at the breath-holding roof scattered with light stars of heaven
Dares not look long but nods to the fresh green marble below him
Thinking that there he sees Thessaly's flower-banked rivers
Washing their gentle way through ripening wheat fields, thick woods,
Shoots twining olive trees, flocks leaping, vines with green tendrils . . .

        ROMANUS's *hymn takes over.*

PAUL   Dark Theban porphyry columns pair in each corner, deep red,
Hewn down from Baalbek's temple, trees made of stone for a great Queen,
Antony gave to the desert to honour his Cleopatra;
Here they reach up thirty feet, love-formed, now honouring Jesus . . .

        ROMANUS's *hymn takes over.*

PAUL   So through the forty windows that circle the dome's great helmet
Catching the sun every hour of the day, safe light guides the sailor
Ploughing his storm-battered ship through the billows of white raging Pontus.
See! The divine light gleams returning its gift from the day's break . . .

        ROMANUS's *hymn takes over.*

SCENE SEVEN

THEODORA
Your husband will have lost weight; but not only
Is the long siege of Rome by Vitiges
Broken, but Belisarius has starved
Ravenna to submission.

ANTONINA
                     He will bring
The Gothic king captured in chains to us,
The keys of Rome jangling from his proud neck.

THEODORA
I'm told King Vitiges with all his staff
Offered the crown to Belisarius—
Of Italy, if he'd renounce his oath
To our Imperial throne.

ANTONINA
                     It's true, they did,
And he duplicitously dandled them
Upon his knee until Ravenna's gates
Flung open for his entry, no blood shed,
No buildings spoiled, the Roman fleet waved in
To Classis harbour with grain and relief.
Large Gothic wives, who sat above the gate
Watching the entry of the Roman ranks,
Spat on surrendering husbands for their fear
Of such small, so few, southern conquerors.
Only when all Ravenna was controlled
Did he in the large public square demand
Their loyal oath to great Justinian.

THEODORA
I hear some Generals were not so loyal;
Taunted he'd rather be a slave than king.

ANTONINA
My husband is a General of genius,
But not an Empire's ruler; not a traitor.

THEODORA
My Antonina, he does all things well.
Now, your advice. I've not been feeling well.

Byzantium

You know how long I spend in the warm bath—
And yet baths frighten me, in spite of guards.
Some cancer seems to pain and aggravate
That area we used to sell for cash.
Could it be God is guiding me to help
Our poorer sisters?

ANTONINA
                       Brothel-keepers search
Out poor homes and, for a few coins, take girls
From willing parents, under oath.

THEODORA
                             I've forced
That practice out of business; set all free.
Each girl's entitled to one set of clothes
And one nomisma from my treasury.
I've also culled in all the Forum nymphs
(Some of them not so young; the sort who charge
Three obols—barely coin enough to live)
And housed five hundred of them on that shore
In an old palace, now endowed by me,
The Convent of Repentance.

ANTONINA
                       What a laugh!
We need more nuns as teachers. You do care
For girls in poverty. Some will object.

THEODORA   Too many die too young, while men grow fat.

ANTONINA   Like Cappadocian.

THEODORA
                    Call the lawyers in!
I'll leave. Perhaps it's better if I know
Less than a babe unblemished.

Exit THEODORA.

Act Two

SCENE EIGHT

Enter TRIBONIAN, AGATHIAS, *and* LYDUS.

ANTONINA Tribonian. You are distinguished now,
Patrician Master of the Laws; and loyal.
Agathias, I hear you now keep
A diary like Procopius. And Lydus—
You married a rich wife, and will receive
A panegyric from the Emperor.
All three of you are experts in the law.
All three have much to lose if treason strikes.
Will you swear now an oath, on your damnation,
To record faithfully the words you hear
And take them to the Emperor? Will you
Tribonian? By the Almighty God?

TRIBONIAN I swear.

ANTONINA And Agathias too?

AGATHIAS I swear.

ANTONINA And you, John Lydus?

LYDUS I swear that I shall.

ANTONINA All three of you hang in perpetual flames
If you go back on one straw of your oath.
Hide behind this, and do not move or breathe.

They hide. Enter COMITO.

COMITO John Cappadocian is here. He asks:
'Are you alone?'

ANTONINA Tell him I am.

COMITO I will.

Exit COMITO. *Enter* CAPPADOCIAN.

CAPPADOCIAN Antonina; will you on your soul's
Salvation, as you cry to avoid hell's
Macabre and endless tortures, burning through

Byzantium

All hope that time may pass and bring an end,
And as you pray despair will never dance
On your damnation, where a gulf is fixed
Between the Prince of Hatred's welcome and
Abraham's bosom in the light of God;
In the full knowledge fiery torments wait
To pluck your limbs and dislocate all peace
For ever in your heart; by Christ do you
Vow that no treachery is here for me?

ANTONINA
By all the saints that cherish round the throne
Of the High Ruler of the universe
The lights that honour him and keep him warm,
By every song that ever angel sang
In rhapsody upon the eternal waves,
By every psalm that shepherd David danced
With all his might before the Ark of God
Which shout and trumpet brought rejoicing
   home,
By the eternal wheels that bear our doom,
By that great day of wrath the mountains fear,
I vow no treachery is here for you.

CAPPADOCIAN This on the Gospels?

ANTONINA   On the Gospels, too.

CAPPADOCIAN I have a daughter whom I love, whom you
Befriended. She whispered to me your words:
Justinian is weak on gratitude
For all your husband has achieved for him—
The captured kings, the brimming treasures, spoil
Of half a world; that, if you had support,
Some things might change.

ANTONINA   Speak on. None hear but us.

CAPPADOCIAN Like Saul I visit sorcerers; like him
For me they give birth to the future, tell
I shall be clothed in purple of Augustus.

ANTONINA Will you perfect a plot to ease of life
Justinian and his Theodora?

Act Two

CAPPADOCIAN   Yes,
I have already thought about our plans,
And we can euthanase the stag-beetle.
He trusts me. What's that sound? My
    bodyguards!
Your oath hurls you to Satan on black wings!

Bodyguards of CAPPADOCIAN *rush in and arrest him.*

TRIBONIAN   The case is clear. A guardian angel sings.

Exeunt.

SCENE NINE

JUSTINIAN   When trouble hits one like an ostrich-kick,
Its eggs innumerable hatch in sand
All round.

MENANDER   I saw the comet! Like a swordfish
Or bearded star, racing from west to east!

JUSTINIAN   It's not the comet but the scourge of Huns
Right on the suburbs of Byzantium.
They've destroyed all from the Ionian Gulf,
Taken the Chersonesus, scaling the walls
On the Black Gulf.

MENANDER   At Thermopylae
I hear they used the path that Xerxes found
On *our* Leonidas; and all are killed.

JUSTINIAN   Chosroes has invaded Syria
Where the long, swaying camel caravans
Thirst across trackless sands to Antioch.
He offered terms, but the Antiochenes
Jeered from the walls, and threw down farce and
    taunts,
Aiming their arrows at his peacemaker.
The soldiers—and Commander—fled the gates
Panicked, outnumbered. Chosroes did not chase.

Byzantium 61

> But our young Blues and Greens stayed for the
>   fight
> With only rocks and sheer exuberance;
> Like storks at snakes, efficient and precise,
> They killed with glee, gave a triumphant shout:
> 'Long live Justinian!' The Persian king
> Burned out our rebuilt Eastern paradise.

ANTONINA *waits*.

Antonina, come in. Is my wife there?

ANTONINA She's resting.

JUSTINIAN Have you news?

ANTONINA To warm your joy.
My Belisarius writes: 'The Imperial Church
You dreamed to lift Ravenna's soul to God
In firm obedience, with triumphal arch
Crowned by the head of Christ, your dolphins
    round,
Stands in completed majesty.'

JUSTINIAN Are the
Mosaics of my wife and me in place?

ANTONINA He who in fear steps through the arch sees up
High on the starry summit of the vault
Before the altar, the white Lamb of God,
Spotless, all walls glowing beneath him: who
Hesitates further blinks the Eastern apse,
Holiest of Holies—Christ on a blue globe,
Beardless, a young Apollo, archangels
And saints attend him. On each wall below,
Facing each other, your two portraits stand,
Earth's representatives of Heaven's command.

JUSTINIAN No church should take more than five years to
    build;
But this exceeds our high and fluttering hopes.

ANTONINA	Now that all Italy—Ravenna, Rome— Is yours, please may I have my husband home?
JUSTINIAN	We need him. Persia's dishonoured our peace. Antioch's sacked; the Huns are at our gates . . . I'll make economies. The Consulship, For one, can go! It is abolished. Where Is Cappadocian?
ANTONINA	He is under guard For planning Theodora's death—and yours.

Enter TRIBONIAN, AGATHIAS, *and* LYDUS, *followed by*
CAPPADOCIAN *under guard.*

JUSTINIAN	(*Reading the charge*) Tribonian, Agathias, Lydus did You witness this?
ALL THREE	We did.
JUSTINIAN	What can you say?
CAPPADOCIAN	A crawling worm, a poisoned arrow-head, A haggish putrefaction painted on A skull, the daughter of mendacity, A baited trap perfumed with blasphemy, Stairway to Satan's kingdom, is a woman. This Antonina . . .
JUSTINIAN	I know what she did. You've been a fool. We have been friends. I will Not torture nor impale you. Be a priest! Your property comes to the Treasury For public use.
CAPPADOCIAN	I will not be a priest!
JUSTINIAN	You shall. Come! Shave his head outside. Take him To arrest in Propontis Cyzicus. The Bishop there will train you every day: But never come within my sight again.

SCENE TEN

PAUL: The Persian ambassador for the Emperor!

Enter ISDIGOUSNAS.

JUSTINIAN: Isdigousnas! Welcome to our home!

ISDIGOUSNAS: Chosroes, Emperor of Emperors,
Lord of the Rising Sun, to Justinianus
Flavius Caesar, of the Setting Moon;
Brothers from ancient time, each sworn to help
Other at need, with men or money. Here
I bring you gifts, and, from the King of Kings
A letter.

JUSTINIAN: King of Kings, and Lord of Persia
In whose name you stand here—a brother's welcome!
(*Reads*) This letter asks if I'm enjoying health.
Is that all?

ISDIGOUSNAS: What else matters between friends?

JUSTINIAN: Your king has ransacked, burned, destroyed, and raped
Our greatest Eastern city, Antioch.

ISDIGOUSNAS: A slight misunderstanding. He has built
Another Antioch by Ctesiphon,
And settled all the captive citizens,
Giving them baths, so they may feel at home;
A Hippodrome, where he supports the Greens;
And sanctuary for all Roman slaves
Related to Old or New Antiochenes.
One can't do more than that.

JUSTINIAN: Isdigousnas,
They have become his subjects!

Act Two

ISDIGOUSNAS   Privileged,
Under no magistrates, but him alone.
They feed entirely at the State's expense:
Called 'The King's People'.

JUSTINIAN   Magnanimous indeed!
Those kings who treat divine things with respect
When cause for war arises use their power
And friendship to ward off catastrophe.
Those are the wise. The foolish lightly bring
Heaven's curse down on them for creating war
On empty pretexts, for no cause but greed.
It is not difficult to destroy peace;
But to restore serenity again,
When no man knows the outcome, is not easy.
What pain and grief, what sins must be endured
If we unleash the leopards of destruction
At our two throats! You took our gold for peace,
And spend it massacring our Roman towns.

Enter COSMAS.

I know I am accessible, but this
Is monstrous!

COSMAS   Mighty Emperor; my Lord,
Forgive me. I must speak to you . . .

JUSTINIAN   Who let
Him in?

PAUL   I did, most mighty Emperor.

ISDIGOUSNAS   How interesting! One request I have
From King Chosroes, who loves all his flock,
Any of whom can come at any time
To him. All fighting's ceased now . . .

JUSTINIAN   Lazica?
If Persia wins at Colchis, nothing will
Prevent you sailing all the Euxine Sea

Byzantium

And gnawing at our stomach! One of your flock,
Nachoragan, your General—a good man—
He summoned from Iberia, neatly incised,
And ripped off in one piece, down to his feet,
His skin, his body printed in reverse
On it. Then blew it up, like a wineskin,
And swung it from a pole.

COSMAS   High politics!
Emperor, I must see you; but with him
Around I can't say what I must!

JUSTINIAN   Then wait!
What was your king's request?

ISDIGOUSNAS   For treasured gold,
If you can spare some; in return for peace.
The King of Kings has not been well. Will you
Lend him a Roman doctor, Tribunus,
Who cured him once before?

JUSTINIAN   Of course I will!

ISDIGOUSNAS And seven philosophers from Athens have
Sought refuge with our philosophic king,
Feeling your prohibition of their gods
On high Olympus made us more attractive.
They now wish to return. Will you, on oath,
Persecute them no longer? Let them go
Back to their homes to worship there in peace?

JUSTINIAN Provided they do not corrupt the young . . .

COSMAS Emperor . . .

ISDIGOUSNAS   A truce to search for peace?

JUSTINIAN A truce in which hostilities all cease!
We'll meet at banquet.

Exit ISDIGOUSNAS.

Act Two

You disgraced yourself.
The fate of nations turned on what we said.

COSMAS — I'm sorry, but these silkworms' eggs won't live
Much longer without skilled attention.

JUSTINIAN — Eggs!

COSMAS — Yes; in this stick. My two monks carried it
From China.

JUSTINIAN — Quick! Take anything you need!
Our own silk industry! Just make them breed.

Exeunt.

SCENE ELEVEN

COMITO — Has your black crab eased paining?

THEODORA — Yes; I think so.
Keep me informed, now that I'm weak and can
Do little. What of Photius?

COMITO — Trouble there.
Antonina, as you know, has fallen
In love with her own godson, Theodosius,
And is promiscuous in front of all.
Photius her son is jealous.

THEODORA — So he is.
It's semi-sibling rivalry. I've found—
By systematic torture of him—where
Photius locked up Theodosius:
Safe in a prison in Cilicia.
He took his flogging bravely. A surprise
Awaits our lusty lady.

COMITO — Dearest sister,
The bramble habits scratched by us when young

| | Fester our undersides, and bruise to bud
White flowers above, but fruits with purple bloom
Beneath, when ripeness comes; like dewberries. |
|---|---|
| THEODORA | It's true. Do you remember us when young?
You were the best of all child prostitutes,
And I walked with you, carrying your stool,
Dressed as a slave girl in a small sleeved frock. |
| COMITO | And when our father died, when I was six
And you were four, mother married again
Another circus-trainer, who could help
With animals and striptease? We were Greens,
The poorer faction, then! Chief dancing-master
Asterius blocked his appointment so
Some friend could buy the job? |
| THEODORA | Though I was small,
I can remember mother's tears; her strength
That day she plaited flowers round our heads,
Made us carry a posy in each hand
We were to hold up as we were paraded
As suppliants, in front of a vast, mocking
Hippodrome crowd, before a race began. |
| COMITO | How our Green faction spat and jeered at us? |
| THEODORA | Led by Asterius, no doubt. |
| COMITO | The Blues
Who had a sudden vacancy showed pity, |
| THEODORA | And earned my eternal gratitude. |
| COMITO | And made
Our stepfather the Keeper of the Bears. |
| THEODORA | Antonina! Come in. |

Enter ANTONINA.

Act Two

> Dearest Patrician,
> A pearl fell into my hands yesterday—
> The most attractive ever seen. Would you
> Like just a glimpse?

ANTONINA   A pearl? Of course, my Queen.
Cheer me. I'm grieving for my lost strong boy.

THEODORA   Your lost strong boy? Your lover-godson?

ANTONINA   Yes.
Soothe me with oyster's irritation, long
Our coveted beauty.

THEODORA   It's unique; and yours.
Look through that window.

ANTONINA   Theodosius!

COMITO   Why don't you speak?

ANTONINA   Goodness incarnate,
        Queen
Of marvellous generosity, my patron,
Protectress, Empress, friend!

THEODORA   He will live here
In safety. There's a room set for you both.
My husband will make him a General
If I have my way. Yes—go and enjoy him.

Exit ANTONINA.

COMITO   Does Belisarius know?

THEODORA   He's due back soon.
I wish I had her passion! But I'm weak,
And never since we married been unfaithful.

COMITO   You have been generous. Lie now, and sleep.
                Exeunt.

SCENE TWELVE

JUSTINIAN: As our great prisoner accepts the faith
Of Athanasius, unlike Gelimer,
I give him lands in Asia, and make
The King a Senator and a Patrician.
I have already abolished the Consulship;
And though you have, now, brought two captive kings
Before my throne: Gelimer, Vitiges:
The Vandal monarch and the Gothic crown,
There cannot be a second Triumph.

BELISARIUS: Lord
Emperor, I am happy and satisfied
To have the substance, not the ceremony,
Of true achievement. It means more to me
That in the harbour where Ravenna's Goths
Waved in our fleet unharmed, there stands a church
That honours you, God's regent here on earth.
Not the imposing grandeur of your own
Imperial Church of Italy; not that.
Just a basilica where light and grace
Dance up twelve perfect columns, over wind-
Swept acanthus leaves carved in white marble, to
The mosaic apse, where all your flock, as sheep
In a green flowering meadow rich with trees,
Look up to blessing from the saint.

JUSTINIAN: The marble?

BELISARIUS: Matchless, from Proconnesus.

JUSTINIAN: They offered you
The crown of Italy, if you would raise
Your legions' standards against me.

BELISARIUS: They did.

JUSTINIAN   And did you toy with infidelity?

BELISARIUS   Only to save blood on both sides; a ruse.

JUSTINIAN   How do I know?

BELISARIUS   Why, look! Because I'm here!

JUSTINIAN   I've passed a law that no arms may be sold
                   To private individuals; and that
                   As all of us are frail, we mitigate
                   Corporal punishment slightly to forbid
                   The cutting off of both hands or both feet.
                   For theft, no maiming now. To please my wife,
                   No women go to prison any more;
                   Just to a nunnery, to keep them chaste.
                   Such things should make us loved . . .

BELISARIUS   My lord, you are!

JUSTINIAN   And yet conspiracies cobra up their heads.
                   Our acts of conquest decimate the race,
                   And sometimes those we freed are wholly ruined.

BELISARIUS   My orders were to win the provinces
                   So that the Empire's strong, and is restored
                   To all it stretched before Honorius.
                   Didn't Saint Sabas promise you just that?
                   You have the energy, and the persistence
                   That a successful General counts upon
                   Back home.

JUSTINIAN   This isn't Old Rome born again,
                   But a Romano-Greek precariousness
                   Which you, Tribonian, Anthemius, Procopius,
                   With half a dozen other men of genius,
                   Create, proclaim, restore, record, defend
                   As my world. What when all of us are gone?
                   Are we Time's millionaires, inheritors
                   Of Rome, indeed, but in a Christian spirit?

We are part of an age, perhaps, that's passing;
The last great flowering before the night.
Bear with me. My wife's strength fades. I am ill.
Black plague sweeps up from Egypt. Beirut's buried
By a huge earthquake: all the glory of
The Law—the young men, teachers, libraries—
Crushed into dust and blown through windswept fires.
The mighty *Code* and *Digest* of Rome's law,
Our masterpiece, was only just in time.
Now to root out heresy and schism
That vulture Christ's beatitude, draw up
And clarify true doctrine for the Church.

SCENE THIRTEEN

Enter PROCOPIUS.

Procopius. You have recorded all
Our Belisarius has achieved and won.
Will you bring me your diaries?

PROCOPIUS   Emperor.
All that I have is yours. The plague is here
Spreading each hour. Your modest diet saves
Your divine greatness. Others feel a slight
Fever at first, no more. Some lassitude
Till evening; nothing much. Then suddenly
Round armpits, in the groin, beneath the ears
Black pustules large as kitchen lentils break.
Many cough blood. The bowels are infected.
Baths help; but in a day or two breath stops.

JUSTINIAN   What can we do?

PROCOPIUS   Women seem less affected,
Though many die. The graves are over-full.
Uncared-for bodies sprawl the weeping streets
In putrefaction that's spread by the wind.

Act Two

JUSTINIAN
: Order the magistrates to arrange carts,
Ringing a bell, to gather up all bodies,
And bury them in pits beyond our walls.
Menander!

Enter MENANDER.

    Organize the Blues and Greens
To clear the bodies from the homes. I'll pay
Them richly.

PROCOPIUS
:   All the shops and trades have closed.
Starvation spectres us. We must have bread.

JUSTINIAN
: Is the Basilica water cistern clean?

PROCOPIUS
: That masterpiece keeps drinking water pure.

BELISARIUS
: My men will search for food to feed the city.

JUSTINIAN
: Please see they do. What is that noise again?

Enter PAUL.

PAUL
: The tremors of the earth have hurled the dome
Of Saint Sophia, and Anthemius
Is dead! Tribonian dies of the plague.
Our Lydus tends and comforts him, but he,
Too, feels the bursting horror in the groin.

JUSTINIAN
: No more!
Pestilence, famine, earthquake, threats of war—
Why, the four horsemen of the apocalypse
Ride on this city!

PROCOPIUS
:   A deserted orphan
I saw being suckled by her pet she-goat.

JUSTINIAN
: We live our lives by faith in spiders' webs.
God knows our moment of departing. Come!
Have soldiers ready, Belisarius.
Search out food, but prepare to ambush Huns

And hurl the plague to their swift Cotrigurs.
A burning ship at night on shoreless sea
Is not so hopeless as we seem to be.
Out! And to work! I'll will all to be well!

Exeunt all except JUSTINIAN.

SCENE FOURTEEN

Enter THEODORA.

JUSTINIAN   My Theodora?

THEODORA   May I be with you?
Alone? I'm near the end, and need your love.

JUSTINIAN   The plague? No, that old crab, the growing cancer
Has gripped you hard.

THEODORA   And I can fight no more.
Will you, when I go, think about the poor?
Remember your own home; your uncle's, too—
A farmer's boy from Thrace? Now you are Prince
Of all the world. From those whom much is given,
God will require much. Baptize the Nubians.
Prepare another Ecumenical Council
To celebrate the end of Gothic war.
Bring unity, and peace; and, always, build.

JUSTINIAN   My love, for whom all Empire has been won—
Stay! Fight for life!

THEODORA   Leisure, and elegance,
Patrician virtues you have always scorned,
Accompany us to the funeral.

JUSTINIAN   No more of that: your priest will soon be here.
My active military days taught me

Act Two

                The difference between a perfect body,
                Beautiful, dead, complete, and one live bird
                In flight is infinite.

THEODORA   Yes, infinite.
                My coming terror shall not make you afraid.
                See how my soul swims like a nimbus cloud!
                When old men saw me they stood up, and kings
                Stopped talking, to lay fingers on their mouths.
                I am a rainbow burning into mist,
                And, as the daylight tiptoes from the dusk,
                Soft, heavy wings beat over my head's nest.
                I must rest, Emperor. (*Dies*)

JUSTINIAN   How could you! God protect you in your flight!
                And may that leafy avenue of limes
                Where truth is lived, not learnt, be yours tonight.
                You've closed the window to my soul, where air
                And laughter will not come again.

                Enter COMITO.

                                      Don't cry.
                Our offspring was the Empire. What am I?
                A celibate singing a lullaby.

                      END OF ACT TWO

EPILOGUE

AGATHIAS *alone*.

For seventeen more years Justinian
Lived on, a widower preoccupied
With Church affairs of State. When he had gone,
Quietly, one night in his bed, two years
Was all it lasted—till his vast Empire,
Restored, began its long disintegration.
Plague and old age took our friends. Antonina
Repented her last years and fortune in
A convent. Theodora? Venerated.
The languages we speak, laws we respect;
That shaping infancy of all our thought
In Athens' temples, agora, and groves
Admired by Rome's young republic; our
    bequeathed
Legacy from the House of Caesar; all
That flowered into Christianity
Would have been lost, irrevocably, blown
Out with the dust of thought. Justinian,
Not understanding, passed it on to us
In stone, mosaics, buildings, ivories,
Above all words, and love—Time's enemies;
For great men are not always wise. Call him
Sinister, if you will; a good perceiver
Of others' genius. Now all is done
In our Byzantium of Justinian.

FINIS

Oxford's Gift to Cambridge

Review by His Honour Judge Colin Kolbert,
Law Fellow at Magdalene College, Cambridge,
and translator of Justinian for the 'Penguin Classics'.

THE STAGE, 3.v.1990

The Oxford University Dramatic Society (OUDS) gave the première of Francis Warner's new play *Byzantium* in King's College Chapel, Cambridge, followed by two performances in the University Church, Oxford, and another in Winchester Cathedral.

Byzantium is a play in two acts. It opens in 527 A.D. with the service in which Justinian is crowned Emperor in succession to his uncle Justin. In Act One Justinian is full of zeal and optimism for the tasks which his vision sets before him. Act Two is altogether more sombre, with unrest at home, news of a catastrophic earthquake at Beirut, and even Byzantium itself plague-stricken and the Empress herself dying. Moreover, the Emperor is plotted against by wily Cappadocian, who is trapped by the spirited Antonina, only to be spared from death by the Christian magnanimity of Justinian.

This complex background is sketched lightly yet comprehensively by Warner in elegant and beautiful verse which was delivered with clarity and fluency by an admirable young cast directed by Tim Prentki.

The text has scholarship, metre and rhythm: the story has drama, intrigue, pace and humour. The writing is spare and the set sparse. The production by OUDS Presidents Louise Chantal and Richard Long, directed by Tim Prentki, achieved miracles of atmosphere with a minimum of props, and the actors were faultless in their lines, vigorous and well-rehearsed.

Despite the youth of them all, they portrayed a wide range of convincing characters. Justinian (Tim Hudson) compelled attention whenever he was on stage, as did his Empress Theodora (Bridget Foreman). The action is held together by the figure of Justinian, even when he is offstage, and Tim Hudson was more than equal to his formidable part. The melodic voice of Dougal Lee's memorable playing of Agathias conveyed all the lyric beauty of his lines to a captivated audience without losing a whit of meaning in the conveyance.

Warner did not choose an easy subject with *Byzantium*. He chose a challenge and he rose to that challenge and surmounted it magnificently. He is a master of plot and characterization and, indeed, of the English language, which he commands with a benign authority and loving finesse.